AMERICAN PURGATORY

AMERICAN PURGATORY

Rebecca Gayle Howell

WINNER
The Sexton Prize
for Poetry 2016

EYEWEAR PUBLISHING

First published in 2017
by Eyewear Publishing Ltd
Suite 333, 19-21 Crawford Street
Marylebone, London W1H 1PJ
United Kingdom

Cover design and typeset by Edwin Smet
Author photograph by Matt White
Printed in England by TJ International Ltd, Padstow, Cornwall

ISBN 978-1-911335-44-3

*Eyewear wishes to thank Jonathan Wonham for his
generous patronage of our press.*

*The editor has generally followed American spelling and punctuation
at the author's request.*

WWW.EYEWEARPUBLISHING.COM

For Alicia Ostriker,
who showed me a
way back to faith.

REBECCA GAYLE HOWELL
is the author of *Render/
An Apocalypse* and the translator
of Amal al-Jubouri's *Hagar Before
the Occupation/Hagar After
the Occupation*, both of which
received wide critical acclaim.
Native to Kentucky, Howell
is a senior editor for the
Oxford American.

The Sexton Prize
for Poetry 2016

EYEWEAR PUBLISHING

FINAL JUDGE'S CITATION

The title of Rebecca Gayle Howell's *American Purgatory* – like the book itself – is surprising in its juxtapositions. One thinks more of the geography of Dante than that of the United States when we think of the condition or place of being spiritually purified. Moreover, as the epic poet made clear, purgation is a state of temporary expiation: we are purged from sin on our way to another, presumably better, place. But where might that be? In Howell's haunting and distinctive vision of the American South 'No one was born here. We are persons held to service and labor,' condemned to suffering a precarious, dangerous landscape replete with worms, snakes, dust, drought, and wind. There's work, and then more work to be done, in awful circumstances; yet fishing in dry rivers is somehow possible, thirsty weeds of cotton manage to straggle and grow. Amid the moon lowering and dogs barking, there remains prophecy, and stories get told. There may be groans instead of song, humming rather than intelligible words, but the stories get told, and Howell tells them, too – unforgettably and redemptively – with grace, eyes open. 'We reap,' she assures us with glimmers of hope, 'What we show.'

Don Share

TABLE OF CONTENTS

IT'S LIKE THIS

No one was born here. We are persons held to service and labor. We are the ones keeping it going. And under us, others keep us going.

They say when all this was grass, you might dig down a foot, but you'd find moist dirt. That some worm would be there to eat what rots, to resurrect with shit our humus. When it's dry a worm will cocoon, take care of itself, curl tight in its tear of mucus until the sand is soil again. Snakes is what we have. Maybe I don't know what forgiveness is, but I know a snake will unhook its own jaw to get what's there to take.

This isn't about the snakes. When I was a child I fought like a child. I wiggled out of any strong arm trying to hold me, hold on to me. I was afraid of my brevity I know now. The woman's shadow I called *Mother* cast so long, I could not see her eyes and felt she did not end. She did. When she was gone, I'd hide on the stairs and sit silent as evening reached through a row of square windows each no bigger than my palm. I'd press my face hard against the cool iron rail and count the specks suspended in the light's amber.

The dust here is big. And when it's windshot, it gets in. My eyes, my teeth, the bed, where I sweat out the childish things. We work a whore's hours, but care less. Exterminate. Landscape. Fire watch. Pave the lots. Cut hair. Bartend. Plumb. Morning comes early, and so do we, a mess of women and men in yesterday's clothes, made to compete for work we'll be made to do. Get your I.D. *Number two forty-four. Number one hundred-*

eight. Number Idontgiveagoodgoddamn because they're not calling me anyway. The best job is laying fence. Everybody wants a fence. Some, so close it's like we're planting the posts right through the middle of their feet. Hang a sign that reads *Don't Tread On Me.*

Take this dog. One of a dozen laid low by some cargo truck trying to make his hour count. I'm supposed to shovel it, her and the rest. When I look behind me, the day lines the road's shoulder with black trash bags that shine in the heat like water shines when you want to get in it. The traffic moves. Between it and the wind, I plant my feet to bend but not fall into her. I'll have to break her legs so I can fit her into the bag. I'm given so many bags.

That's the way with drought: nobody wants to be where she is. We've built an offing of shopping plazas. We live in trailers then tell ourselves they'll stand. And outside town, it isn't a town, the cotton fields, plowed neat, ready as a girl. The thing about dogs is they need us. Otherwise they're halfanimals, scabbed with mange, scared of the high sun. I can see why. What do I know about drought. What do I know about winds that open the plain sky, the sun bleeding into blue hour when the burrow owls rise up to stalk, their eyes warning fires, what do they know. Here's something to cry about: it's a myth. No such thing as a good bitch without a bad bitch. Dogs are gods only so far as they can't help what they are. I can lie. I can lie my way straight through the fat belly of fear. But I can't help that, I'm here.

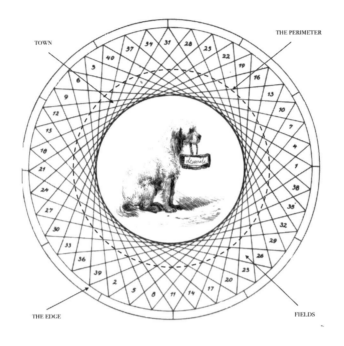

THE PERIMETER

TOWN

THE EDGE

FIELDS

Map #1: Bird's Eye View
(desecrate)

13

WE DO NOT KNOW WHAT WE DO NOT KNOW

The drops sound like rocks thrown into a steel tub;
a window glass taps, *Not today. Not today.*
Dust to mud, the crew and I lay sod
and expect New England. I should listen.
My grace is sufficient, Brother Slade reminds us.
He and I take off our shoes and stand bowed,
washing. He is tall for a Bible man, and with red hair.
The air is almost oceanic. I do not trust him.
Everything dies, I tell him an old lover said that
to me each night. Slade rises to bend backward,
his hand on his hip, his eyes open straight to the sun.

EVERY JOB HAS A FIRST DAY

Slade was pulling minnows out of the dry river
the day we met. Puddles, more or less, was all
that was left. But what could live wanted to and
tried, treading narrow circles, a glide of brittle fins.
He wore those rubber boots, though the sun was
an anvil, and very little wet; he smiled, I remember
that, his nickel smile right at me, his fingers
letting fall the small fishmuscles into a bag filled
with yellow tap. I didn't ask his name, or what
it was he thought he was doing, but we talked,
I listened as he taught me to relax the hand, just
enough. They can smell, he said, the oils our pores
release when we tense to catch. You have to believe it,
he said. You don't mean any harm.

I'M COVERED IN IT RIGHT NOW

All we grow here is cotton stalks. Thirsty weed
that sells. When summer leaves, look out:
the high ground will be fogged by bolls
the size of testicles, every inch; a reap of what
we have for what we want; of what we want.
Thirsty, but it sells. The enginepickers would lift
three, four rows, the heads and the seeds. Now
it's all handwork: pull the lint pure. Quiet,
the labor; quiet the greed. Today I watched
a mother and son shop the market. The Kid led
that tired woman like she wore a leash. Last night,
the fox traded his hollow for two rats. Before that,
the rats ate trash because it's all we had. Commerce.
Every action, exchange. With cotton you can stuff
your white ears white. You can swaddle your tongue
dumb. Do you understand? I mean to explain
the high demand.

I'LL SPARE YOU THE DETAILS

We treat them like it's catching, like those people
chose a joke birthright. Some have no eyes,
the sockets patched with paper flesh; others, gifted –
three arms, four, an ear. The Kid is one.
His just-born heart thrummed outside his body,
no breastbone, his mouth red-wide for the surging
scream, but silence is what was heard, save the swish
of lifeblood through the Brutechild's valves,
bulbous wet root meant hidden all his days
there exposed like a woman to the air's sting,
like the woman who lay beneath him, dead – no,
struck at what she'd made. Most Brutes are put
to work the fields, bent over their secrets; swollen heads
bobbing in and out the rows. The spray planes still circle
on the hour. I don't know what the pilots think
there's left to kill. It's not true: some were born here.
It's that no one gives birth here anymore.

SAME SONG SECOND VERSE

I get sick when I see one of their stubarms waving.
I don't want to touch them, and anyway Slade hurries us
when we're told to go log stock – who could report
what those people need. The planes sprayed for weevils,
that's what was said, then fire ants, that's what was said,
but it was a tent city of mounds today. Scamp pests
will eat any flesh. The air rots out there. I'd blame
the Brutes, but I know it's my own dread I smell
fetid and kicking. The ones who have tongues
confess toward night – *It was grace that taught my heart
to fear. And grace my fears relieved. How precious
did that grace appear. The hour I first believed*. I think
it's about regret, being wrong, the way things first appear.

TRY TO SEE NO EVIL

From a distance the brushfire looked like veins crossing,
a flame's thin arm, like electric wires, like Christmas.
Cigarette ash, a spot of grass; I swear my breath sparked.
Sometimes I dream the ground approaches, a soil
of copper snakes, tongues pronged as divining rods
splitting the air. Last night two diamondbacks, a cross
of tails bent to the motion of a clock. They moved down
my neck. I woke cold and sweating. I woke knowing
I had no home. They say the low moon is coming.
Maybe so. Why else would the street dogs make so much
noise. I wish it meant something. I wish a moon could pull
so strong dirt would gush a well. I'd get my silver bucket.
I'd open my mouth. The fire – it's a game; one guy sets it
from boredom and from boredom the other puts it out.

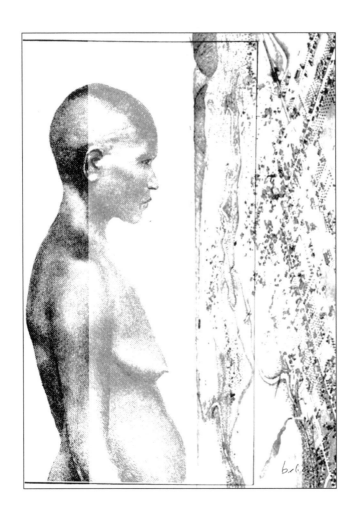

Map #2: Detail Of Town
(believe)

YOU CAN'T TELL THE TRUTH

One of the things we do for pay is count
who's left. Hell's census bureau. People
talk about leaving as if they could walk out
a door. They want to hear what it sounds like.
Few animals make it. The scorpions do okay,
but the big hides need water, and no one shares.
Bodies lie open on routes that lead out,
and the stink carries on the winds. No mistake,
the roads look like spokes cross-pointed
and soaring to the inner hoop of a wheel,
and we keep it in perfect turning. And there is
no wheel.

SEEING IS BELIEVING

It's prophecy, Slade says. *We'll be delivered*
but we must utterly destroy all the places.
I think to what I've read. The heave offering.
Indulgence tax. We're laying street today;
tar can't get hotter. I turn my head, watch
a pregnant bitch five yards off set attack
on the hound who's come sniffing too close.
From this minute's fight, a thin membrane
guards her bloodlitter; her gums, flares,
her sky teeth. I listen. *It's prophecy,* he says
again, because he can.

BELIEVING IS SEEING

The first will be last, says Slade. Then I say,
What first? The last will be last. No lilies
grow in these fields. Consider the cotton,
Slade follows. I do: a verb: to get it, or:
agree. As in: *He cottoned to any story*
he could muster. Or: *She did not cotton*
to his running off at the mouth. You know,
a burrow owl, when in danger, will dig down
and sound a viper's rattle to fool the one
who hunts him, or, at least, fool himself
he's safe. But can he still hear what's come?
We've been called to a place worse than us
to learn there's nothing here worse than us.
I think one day I'll say to Slade, *Slade,*
I've been sent a holy word: Shut up.

IT'S ALL THE SAME

The last will be first, Slade says. The pitch
of his voice river-low, as if he's getting shed
of a remorse, and I can almost not hear him,
but I do. I say, *Could you repeat that?* He says,
The last will be sad. Now that I believe.

THE RISK IS THERE IS NO RISK

The Kid's riding his bike, Fibonacci spiral
in a cement lot. It's hot. I'm in one of the parked cars,
stranded. I don't know where to go. A man with a star
inked on his neck crosses the street toward us.
Five points and patriot blue. He's alone, The Kid.
He knows better. Drink water, but don't drink the water
here, his mother could have said. Above us, geese charge
north on abacus wires strung tight to – what. What sky
are we held by? Who counts our sins.

GRACKLES, TO BE SURE

The birds arrange themselves isosceles.
Two on the ground, one in the lowest branch
of a cedar weed. The first looks up at the second;
the second and third, at each other.
Rat crows. Their aurora borealis bodies.
Their oil-spill down and glint. I hear
they eat trash. I hear they nest in trash.
On my way to the bridge I see them and stop.
Not one of them looks at me. All I can think is
I want one to look at me.

A SHIFT IS OPENING

You get a pick-up, a light, a hand gun,
the wind of a night to drive the perimeter
and precision shoot the dust. The cotton
is young; the jackrabbits are not; the coyote
packs long-since thinned for thirst. Who else
is left to hunt but us? – and if you beat the flies,
the meat is fresh, spiced, almost menthol.
The meat is free. Advertise *Work! No one
at your back. More marks than bullets.*
A rodent famous for sex. Did we think
they'd shoot themselves? The rest of us want to
and can't. But it's over Jordan for them, fields
trenched, stalks coming up. Pleasure don't quit.
I'd sell their severed feet for charms, stitched shut.

I WANT THE SUNDOWN WORK

Slade takes my thin finger and curls it to the trigger,
pushes on me a little to show how it gives then stops.
I feel his chest lift against my back; his breath,
my ear, conch-echo hum, his thumb, my thumb,
handcock the hammer, short-range. As if a pistol
was built to verify – *do you mean it?* Slade does.
He wants me to pull it, *Pull it!* he spits then teases
my finger between his and the lever, the firing pin,
the cartridge, the fire. 10' and a ground squirrel; me.
We detonate. I shake. *Praise!* my hands shake *Praise!*
the Devil. Killing feels so little like dying, praise him
who made it so.

TO BE FAIR

In the gun's sight they look like messengers,
their wingy sacks, regal-white in length,
worn over their bowed backs as to trail
shallow furrows among the stalks well after
the pickers have hobbled through.
I see it now – the herd of it, the rabbits
and Brutes, the arthritic plants,
pestilence – the whole scene breathing
as if with ease, conspired, and no one
could blame me, none worthy would, if I said
out loud, *These reapers might well get what's
coming.* And if they did, they'd carry it home.

DESTROY ALL THE PLACES

The economics will satisfy. One plus one equals
legion. Fight them for a share. Once I had a lover
who taught me right; around my throat he'd clamp
his humid hands, his fingers mashing my pipe,
his mouth shouting words at me; *fault, responsibility*,
I don't remember now, a hundred flags snap
in the wrong winds. Heritage. Best to get up now
and forget; you can erase today if you practice.
I have work to do, but no more hope we make it
out of here than living will let us die. That's what
it means to owe a thing. It means you are owned.
And which are you, now, the owner or the owned.

O MERCY ME

The dirt storms regular now,
as if the downdraft's haul of loose ground
is its own harvest, the wind a blind scythe.
Twilight rides the weather, black-mass
filth, a bulwark full force against the risk
you'll try to see ahead. You don't.
Cars wreck, shop glass breaks.
Stand in the road while the grains spray
your skin scattershot. Your raw eyes.
The day-dark dust does what it wants.
So does the sun. Tomorrow I'll see clear
the fields fenced by old telephone poles.
I'll see Golgotha repeating.

TRY TO HEAR NO EVIL

The old factory's windows were broke out. The inside
gutted. Plaster cracks on the load-bearing walls
snaked under each other exposing the lath beneath,
ordered and nailed. The cladding chipped to
brick and mortar, and where once the roof laid down
rose the branching of chestnut trees, trunks thrusting
up through the concrete floor. I stood, small. I knew
then how much I could not hold. The meeting house.
In the dream I wasn't clear what we'd come to ask for,
but that we'd come, each of our own terror nights,
to say something that could be heard. Once inside,
instead of words, I felt a hum, not a song but a groan,
like the one my mother made when she worked.

LOST AND WON;

Map #3: Detail Of Fields
(reap)

WHAT GOES AROUND

Not all wells are tapped. Some draw sufficient
to run a hose to a house, the low sulfur cloud
a mark of the wetmouth advantaged. As if that's
not enough, they buy the sprays in shades
like police-tape yellow or this-is-not-yours red,
so I can't believe The Kid who, in broad Tuesday light,
slinks under sills to unscrew nozzles and tug
the umbilical weight of rushing water all the way
to his mother's corroded truck bed, where they go
to work. She, bent over like she's burying a sin;
The Kid with arms raised revival, pouring whatever
don't spill at the air into their drought tank.
My mother, hairnet tied fist-tight at the back,
was made to cook; she left early, returned late,
and dark raced dark in her shift. That was the days
of commissaries, when sharing was plenty. The Kid
don't know those days. Love is funny, in that it's dead
but not dead.

GET IT IN YOUR SIGHT

We were at the range to practice shots,
filthy wall of a spot that it is, saccharine
ash air, cut-rate smokes, the plaster's stains
limpid in a way that reminds me of men,
and a throat of a hallway that gulps it all
and us, those black targets, white-line marked
with a circle drawn to the fatal paper heart,
soar above our heads because they've won
death and we haven't, when a guy walks up
to me then past, a look like direction
in his eye, as if he knew a place he wanted
but one I could not see. Slade said
the guy's name was Little. *Little what?* I said,
for meanness, a joke, can't you take a joke,
the man's left hand sunk rotten, I don't know
what else. Little walked right off, deaf
to concern, and I watched Slade watch him
as if he was hunting, but who had the gun.

NO ONE, NOT EVEN ONE

A Brute's as here as the rest of us; feel sorry for.
In the field's store room, you'll find fault.
The ruined ones are souvenirs, spoils,
green jars stinking of preservation, they sit
a stock of bloated, pickled heads, conjoined
tongues, limbless stumps. All eyes open
formaldehyde when any mouth comes talking,
This isn't as bad as it gets. Keep your head down.
Work the double. A wince; is that forgiveness?
Instead I offer a sure pistol grip, squint-aim.
I offer grace. Do you know what it means to be
ashamed? The rubric of fault alters in its shade.
This death preserved in me is well alive; I'd give it
all if I could shut my eyes.

WHO, THEN

When a well does dry up, some people
thirst; others drink dirt. I've got no
argument that draws water but Little does.
He prays with his dowser and complaints,
taking the fight out of a couple of sticks.
Lately I can't wake without seeing him behind
the fueling station or beside the dive bar,
casting his humped shadow on the grease trap,
bent over words I can't hear. Nobody talks
to Little but Little's sure talking to somebody.
Half the time he sinks a pump and right there
our jeremiad washes his soot body, stripped
to the nub like a pruned and fruiting tree.

WHEN YOU'RE WRONG YOU'RE WRONG

Have you been beat? I ask Little. I've got him cornered
at the car lot and he says nothing. Not *no*, nothing,
as if speaking would make it so. I know that sound.
Walking after Little is like walking after me,
like the moon got hung in vain. He's been beat.
The feet heave, the knees break like he's carrying weight.
He's not. All he's got is whatever he don't say. The dead say
they watch their souls leave, mute but not dumb.
Then the eyes close. Water is a ghost. Diviners – it takes
practice to get the target right measured. He's smarter
than a pig, Little, but he's bound.

ONLY HELL HAS NO LIMITS

Slade divines sin with the same precision
as a cowbird takes a shit. *The seed is in those*
witching sticks, the seed is in our want to drink.
I like the way I feel when Little finds a spring.
I think Brutes must be clean: behind my eyes
The Kid is on his bike, ever pedaling to the living
green pond he knows, and it's safe to swim there,
to strip red-naked and sink, to come up for air,
he does not fall from breath, the small wrought fence
fast to his amalgamated heart, he rides as hard
as faith, and I do whatever it takes to follow him,
and the sun does not burn on this day, nothing
burns – none of this story is true, you know.
His mother may not be a Brute, but The Kid knows
what he was born to.

TRY TO SPEAK NO EVIL

The winged car, stranded. The scutch grass
fraught to grow. Hot-polaroid afternoon,
light's filtered wait. Change is certain
except when it's not: Once I saw a twister
of birds, red-eyed raptors, slide along
a hidden helix right down to the white sun.
Here was a thing, I thought, that might
move on.

LET US MAKE MAN IN OUR IMAGE

Stand your ground. We are walking. We are talking now
of the wind. *Defend yourself.* I imagine us a brigade,
the thin three, a gang against the air. I don't know
who taught Slade to run his mouth and Little
to shut his, but there it is. A perfect system.
Slade follows me following Little, his vision
of wells, his fetish, ours. For weeks we've chased
what we want to see. Little stabs the sky like the sky is
a balloon and he's a child playing prank. We aren't kids.

AFTER OUR LIKENESS

When I first found the store-room jars, I saw
my own reflection in the thick glass, my eyes
his eyes, my ears, his absent ear, my periphery
sight wide-net. I felt a heat come to my skin
like danger; I wanted to kill whoever
had killed him, him, her, the bottled up bodies
innocent, the last births. I take my pistol,
aim a passing crow, don't watch where it drops.
Slade talks. Little walks. A gale wind without rain
may be vanity, but you'd be knocked by it.
Two hundred days for profit to ripe, and today
is ripe. A blue asp zigs toward us like a plan.

AND LET THEM HAVE DOMINION

Not like townwork, the fields don't close.
The dogs that have made their way out here
are infested but less afraid. The pickers sleep
among the cotton, wake and watch
for a boll to pop. The sack is endless,
or so it looks now that I'm here stooping in rows
as if I'm low, one of them, a Brute, no, worse,
I'm in the way. In front of me, a picker
without arms, on her knees. She snaps the whole
boll off with her teeth. It ain't her sweet.

OVER EVERY CREEPING THING

Stand your ground. Defend yourself. We are walking.
Slade stops, looks at me; I start. *What do you know?*
Last night I slept in the furrow. He's got what I mean.
I'm ate up with the ants, thirst; my breasts ache,
my blood ended months ago. Little looks on.
We walk between the cotton, the pricks,
and I can't help it. I see all the pickers are girls.
I hear the irrigation sputter on; no one runs for cover.
There is a cistern, Little says.

Map #4: Detail Of Slade's Heart
(please)

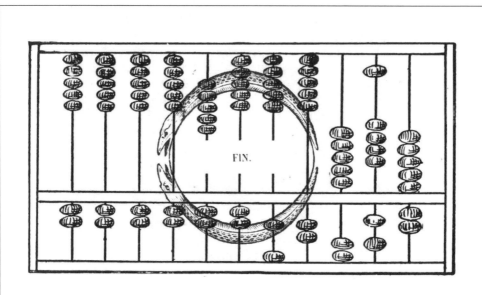

FIN.

please

Map #5: Detail Of Little's Heart
(please)

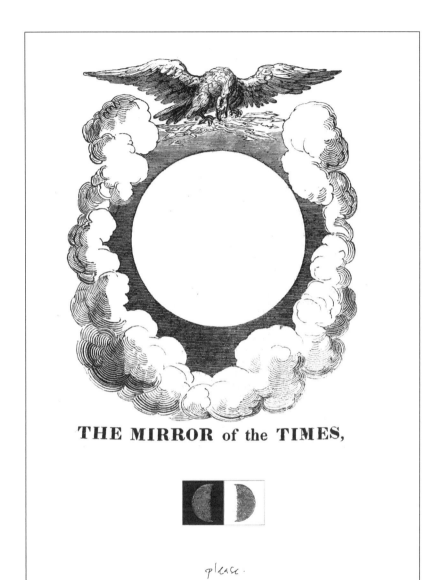

THE MIRROR of the TIMES,

please.

Map #6: Detail Of My Heart
(please)

47

PLEASURE DON'T QUIT

Please that old song screams, and begs me,
Don't go. I hear it in my head in a time
as this, when I am alone, and how *Don't go*
has all my days been my low-ditch song's refrain,
and how I have not known who it was a going,
and how, turns out, it was me. Touch is water,
when it's kind, a cool pool I can drink and sink
down into, resurrect out, rise up, rise up.
But a heat vision won't make it so.

HELL IS EMPTY

I miss Slade most, but more I miss thinking Little
was as good as any, that a body could mean what he says.
Take the fire ant. For every day a queen eggs thousands,
new resined want twisting out of the underground, lined up
with the rest of us, looking for work. I don't know what
I'm looking for. I do wonder if The Kid made it out here,
if he's heard the spray plane over his head shout *Pray for rain*.
If you are blameless, you will be saved. That Kid, his straight-shot
bicycle; no one tried like that Kid. He had no pupils in his eyes,
but who does. I don't blame anyone. We reap what we show.

THE ECONOMICS WILL SATISFY

You'd get signs in town: auto pawn, bail bond, payday
loan, *Give up what you need for want. Don't ask*
the interest rate. The town's time clock will suck your record
right out your hand to punch the day closed. Work for pay,
a real trade. But here, where the sun does not charge
the hour, where all you meet is broke down
but something by might grows, you could trust the dust
may pardon you, you could trust work. Forget cotton.
I'll give you forgiveness: dust to dust. Through the earth's roof
a bullet the speed of my tongue. Hear it: *We are done.*

DIE WHEN YOU DIE

I will fall through a flat glass window
out a shop I wanted to own, and I will scream
a praise chorus to the bare road below.
I will sing. And I will choke, my throat
not strong for singing as it once was
when I was young, but I will scream anyway,
I will choke anyway. And when I hit, I pray
I will be crushed by blind horses once kept
for burden now loosed to their rage,
may the hollow wolves clean up the parade,
but you will not see the flag of warning
I've become, since no one gets out of here
alive, boys, not one.

SOMETHING'S COMING BUT
NEVER DOES

I followed locusts. I thought they were loyal,
but it's a story. In morning's bleached streets
and nights of tungsten glinting, fretted steel legs
ticker minutes past. What did I know, except I needed
a thing to walk behind. The lot tagged *The Devil,*
red spray paint, two concrete steps. This is where I'd go
when the heat came, when no one alive could tell me
how to make the day move on. She lies there, the bitch,
in a bed concave from her weight. Though it was dusk,
I'd see she is the color of dirt. Though fleas opened
new roads through her hair, she'd sleep. I hear thunder.
Some days it rumbles dry, no rain. I'm tired. The air here,
it's like breathing gasoline. I lie down, too. A razor,
a latex glove turned inside out. I curl my body close
to hers, my lips, nose to her spine. I close my eyes.
I want the mites to leave without me, but they don't.

WHO SHALL INHERIT

My mother would say the Devil
impregnates us with each other,
or was it, now, God? The sadness
already inside us, this little light
of mine. She'd also say birth
was a kind of dying, giving birth,
I mean, the womb a catacomb.
Blessed are the poor, the poor,
the poor, the poor, the poor. These
are the thoughts a woman keeps
before she is divided like a judgment.

NOBODY'S DEAD

Slade says he knows his redeemer lives.
To redeem: meaning, to exchange.
My body, promissory note. No thanks.
My left hand has done work. My right,
the nerves run neon-lit into my head.
Slade doesn't know his right from wrong.
Sometimes he looks like a pumpjack,
every minute bowing to what is gone.
Today, I crossed over. You'd think all that
iron and oil would be noisome, and it is.
Loud. I was sick. But I had to walk to the edge
to know the machines surround us,
periphery-blind and working. I'm saying
I got close. And I heard it. The tenorpitch,
a tooth whistle, out from the fault, coming
through us all.

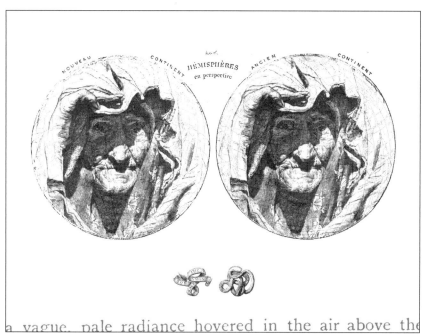

a vague, pale radiance hovered in the air above the

Map #7: Detail Of Extraction
(birth)

EVERYONE WAS BORN HERE

I believed about the cistern, but I didn't
expect the cistern, to find myself
at an opening, a way in, a way out,
I didn't expect to fit, if I tried, shameless,
shimmy to fit. Don't judge. It's how
we got here. You, me, this fetus, this girl,
isn't it every time a girl even when
it's a boy, O the new rooms of rain.
We will float and drink years of rain.
But what I didn't expect were the snakes.
(More than one thing undulates.)
(This is how my water breaks.)

ACKNOWLEDGEMENTS

I am grateful to the following publications for printing this work in sometimes earlier forms:

The Baffler, Blood Orange Review, Guernica, Indiana Review, The Louisville Review, Oxford American, Poetry, Prairie Schooner, Shenandoah, Southern Indiana Review, and *Verse Daily* – also to the editors of the following anthologies for collecting some of these poems: *The Guernica Annual, Hard Lines: Rough South Poetry,* and *The New Farmer's Almanac.*

Without the generosity of The Carson McCullers Center, the Field Office Agency, The Fine Arts Work Center, the Kentucky Arts Council, the Kentucky Foundation for Women, The Oxford American Literary Project, and Texas Tech University this book would not have been written. Thank you for providing the time, space, and support I needed. Your work is God's work.

Likewise, the visual poems enclosed here are largely drawn from one image bank. In 2013, The British Library, in partnership with Microsoft, digitally released millions of colonial-era images to the Public Domain via Flickr Commons. I am no doubt one of countless who will say it: thank you for this openhanded gift.

I am grateful to Curtis Bauer, Maxwell George, and Roger Hodge, the first readers of this work, who lent faith to the poems before the story revealed itself; to Don Share, who believed in the story and the poems; to Frank Giampietro, my first and last editor; and to Kelly Davio, Todd Swift, and all of Eyewear Publishing, for being the best press across two continents.

And to the following, for being close in key moments of this process, my heart: Boogie, Shannon Boyd, Nickole Brown, Kimberly Burwick, Dennis Covington, Arwen Donahue, Kathy Doyle, Liz and Dan Elkinson, Thomas Sayers Ellis, Idoia Elola, Vaughan Ashlie Fielder, Nikky Finney, Boris Fishman, Nick Flynn, Carolyn Forché, Ross Gay, Kevin Goodan, Chloe Honum, Marie Howe, George Jenne, Keith Leonard, Ada Limón, David Lord, Ronni Lundy, Anne Marie Macari, Guy Mendes, Andrew Meredith, Rachel Miller, Matthew Neill Null, Naomi Shihab Nye, Dominic Russ-Combs, Salvatore Scibona, Jacob Shores-Arguello, Jeff Shotts, Savannah Sipple, Emily Smith, Jill and Andy Smith, Stephanie Soileau, Gerald Stern, Jean Valentine, Sarah Wylie and Griffin VanMeter, Matt White, Marcus Wicker, Crystal Wilkinson, Joy Williams, my mother, and Brett Ratliff.

EYEWEAR PUBLISHING

EYEWEAR'S TITLES INCLUDE

EYEWEAR POETRY

KATE NOAKES CAPE TOWN
SIMON JARVIS EIGHTEEN POEMS
ELSPETH SMITH DANGEROUS CAKES
CALEB KLACES BOTTLED AIR
GEORGE ELLIOTT CLARKE ILLICIT SONNETS
HANS VAN DE WAARSENBURG THE PAST IS NEVER DEAD
BARBARA MARSH TO THE BONEYARD
DON SHARE UNION
SHEILA HILLIER HOTEL MOONMILK
MARION MCCREADY TREE LANGUAGE
SJ FOWLER THE ROTTWEILER'S GUIDE TO THE DOG OWNER
AGNIESZKA STUDZINSKA WHAT THINGS ARE
JEMMA BORG THE ILLUMINATED WORLD
KEIRAN GODDARD FOR THE CHORUS
COLETTE SENSIER SKINLESS
ANDREW SHIELDS THOMAS HARDY LISTENS TO LOUIS ARMSTRONG
JAN OWEN THE OFFHAND ANGEL
A.K. BLAKEMORE HUMBERT SUMMER
SEAN SINGER HONEY & SMOKE
HESTER KNIBBE HUNGERPOTS
MEL PRYOR SMALL NUCLEAR FAMILY
ELSPETH SMITH KEEPING BUSY
TONY CHAN FOUR POINTS FOURTEEN LINES
MARIA APICHELLA PSALMODY
TERESE SVOBODA PROFESSOR HARRIMAN'S STEAM AIR-SHIP
ALICE ANDERSON THE WATERMARK
BEN PARKER THE AMAZING LOST MAN
MANDY KAHN MATH, HEAVEN, TIME
ISABEL ROGERS DON'T ASK
REBECCA GAYLE HOWELL AMERICAN PURGATORY
MARION MCCREADY MADAME ECOSSE
MARIELA GRIFFOR DECLASSIFIED
MARK YAKICH THE DANGEROUS BOOK OF POETRY FOR PLANES
HASSAN MELEHY A MODEST APOCALYPSE

EYEWEAR LITERARY CRITICISM

MARK FORD THIS DIALOGUE OF ONE - WINNER OF THE 2015 PEGASUS AWARD FOR POETRY CRITICISM FROM THE POETRY FOUNDATION (CHICAGO, USA).